Ernest Hemingway
(1899 – 1961)

QUOTATIONS
OF
Ernest Hemingway

APPLEWOOD BOOKS
Carlisle, Massachusetts

Ernest Hemingway

ERNEST MILLER HEMINGWAY was born on July 21, 1899, in Oak Park, Illinois, to Clarence and Grace Hemingway. A major American literary figure, Hemingway's works include *A Farewell to Arms* (1929), *For Whom the Bell Tolls* (1940), and *A Moveable Feast* (1964).

Hemingway joined the *Kansas City Star* as a cub reporter at eighteen. During the First World War he volunteered with the American Red Cross and was stationed in Italy. While on canteen duty at the front, he was seriously wounded. He convalesced for six months in Milan, falling in love with his nurse, who rejected him for an Italian officer.

In 1921, Hemingway married Elizabeth Hadley Richardson, with whom he had a son, John. They moved to Paris, where Hemingway freelanced as a foreign correspondent for the *Toronto Star*. Hemingway soon became part of the American expatriate literary community, befriending writers Gertrude Stein, Ezra Pound, F. Scott Fitzgerald, and others. The Hemingways also traveled in Europe, skiing in Austria and attending bullfights in Spain.

The Sun Also Rises (1926) brought critical and popular success. While working on the novel, Hemingway's marriage fell apart. After a divorce in 1927, he married Pauline Pfeiffer. They had two sons, Patrick and Gregory. Based in Key West, Florida, they were often on the move: fishing excursions, hunting in Wyoming, and a safari in Africa.

In 1937, Hemingway returned to Spain to cover the Spanish Civil War for the North American Newspaper Alliance. He composed dispatches in Madrid amid heavy shelling. A supporter of the democratically elected Spanish Republic, his articles openly reflected his sympathies.

Working in Spain alongside him was journalist Martha Gellhorn. After divorcing Pauline, Hemingway married Gellhorn in 1940. They continued their reporting during the Second World War, honeymooning while on assignment in China. Later they both served as war correspondents in Europe, but by then they worked separately. Hemingway observed the Normandy landings on D-day, attached himself to the Twenty-second Infantry Regiment, and saw the liberation of Paris.

After a third divorce, Hemingway married for the fourth time to reporter Mary Welsh in 1946. They lived at La Finca Vigia, Hemingway's home outside of Havana, Cuba. Hemingway was famous for his macho persona, adventurous exploits, and distinctive literary style. In 1952, he won a Pulitzer Prize for his novella *The Old Man and the Sea*. He was awarded the Nobel Prize for Literature in 1954.

Hemingway died in Ketchum, Idaho, on July 2, 1961. He is considered one of the masters of American literature.

QUOTATIONS

OF

Ernest Hemingway

*A*nd how much better to die in all the happy period of un-disillusioned youth, to go out in a blaze of light, than to have your body worn out and old and illusions shattered.
– Letter to his family, Milan, October 18, 1918

*S*ince the good old days when Charles Baudelaire led a purple lobster on a leash through the same old Latin Quarter, there has not been much good poetry written in cafes. Even then I suspect that Baudelaire parked the lobsters with the concierge down on the first floor, put the chloroform bottle corked on the washstand and sweated and carved at the Fleurs du Mal alone with his ideas and his paper as all artists have worked before and since.
– "American Bohemians in Paris," *Toronto Star Weekly*, March 25, 1922

We can't ever go back to old things or try and get the 'old kick' out of something or find things the way we remembered them. We have them as we remember them and they are fine and wonderful and we have to go on and have other things because the old things are nowhere except in our minds now.

– Letter to friend William D. Horne, Paris, July 17–18, 1923

Ernest Hemingway

Bull fighting is not a sport. It was never supposed to be. It is a tragedy. A very great tragedy. The tragedy is the death of the bull.

– "Bull Fighting a Tragedy," *Toronto Star Weekly*, October 20, 1923

Ernest Hemingway

A man's got to take a lot of punishment to write a really funny book.

– Letter to boyhood friend William B. Smith Jr., Paris, December 6, 1924

Y̶ou see I'm trying in all my stories to get the feeling of the actual life across—not to just depict life—or criticize it—but to actually make it alive. So that when you have read something by me you actually experience the thing. You can't do this without putting in the bad and the ugly as well as what is beautiful.

– Letter to his father, Dr. C. E. Hemingway, Paris, March 20, 1925

Ernest Hemingway

M̶y book will be praised by highbrows and can be read by lowbrows. There is no writing in it that anybody with a high-school education cannot read.

– Letter to publisher Horace Liveright, Paris, March 31, 1925

Ernest Hemingway

M̶y attitude towards punctuation is that it ought to be as conventional as *possible*....You ought to be able to show that you can do it a good deal better than anyone else with the regular tools before you have a license to bring in your own improvements.

– Letter to Horace Liveright, Paris, May 22, 1925

*I*t is awfully easy to be hard-boiled about everything in the daytime, but at night it is another thing.
– *The Sun Also Rises*, 1926

Ernest Hemingway

"*H*ow did you go bankrupt?" Bill asked. "Two ways," Mike said. "Gradually and then suddenly."
– *The Sun Also Rises*, 1926

Ernest Hemingway

"*E*veryone behaves badly," I said. "Give them the proper chance."
– *The Sun Also Rises*, 1926

Ernest Hemingway

"*O*h Jake," Brett said, "we could have had such a damned good time together."…"Yes," I said. "Isn't it pretty to think so?"
– *The Sun Also Rises*, 1926

*W*as not referring to guts but something else.
Grace under pressure. Guts never made any money
for anybody except violin string manufacturers.
– Letter to writer F. Scott Fitzgerald, Paris, circa April 20, 1926

Ernest Hemingway

*T*ry and write straight English; never using
slang except in Dialogue and then only when
unavoidable. Because all slang goes sour in a
short time. I only use swear words, for example,
that have lasted at least a thousand years for fear
of getting stuff that will be simply timely and
then go sour.
– Letter to sister Carol Hemingway, Paris, circa October 5, 1929

Ernest Hemingway

*I*f people bring so much courage to this world
the world has to kill them to break them, so of
course it kills them. The world breaks every one
and afterward many are strong at the broken
places. But those that will not break it kills. It
kills the very good and the very gentle and the
very brave impartially. If you are none of these
you can be sure it will kill you too but there will
be no special hurry.
– *A Farewell to Arms*, 1929

"*N*o, that is the great fallacy: the wisdom of old men. They do not grow wise. They grow careful."
– Count Greffi, *A Farewell to Arms*, 1929

Ernest Hemingway

*E*veryone writes prose badly to start but by continuing some get to write it well. Stop or go on is the only advice I know.
– "Statement on Writing," *Modern Writers at Work*, 1930

Ernest Hemingway

*E*schew the monumental. Shun the Epic. All the guys who can paint great big pictures can paint great small ones.
– Letter to editor Maxwell Perkins, Key West, January 5–6, 1932

Ernest Hemingway

*R*emember to get the weather into your god damned book—weather is very important.
– Letter to writer John Dos Passos, Key West, March 26, 1932

There are no subjects I would not jest about if the jest were funny enough (just as, liking wing shooting, I would shoot my own mother if she went in coveys and had a good strong flight).

– Letter to *New Yorker* critic Robert M. Coates, Nordquist Ranch, Wyoming, October 5, 1932

Ernest Hemingway

"Madame, all our words from loose using have lost their edge."

– *Death in the Afternoon*, 1932

Ernest Hemingway

There is no lonelier man in death, except the suicide, than that man who has lived many years with a good wife and then outlived her. If two people love each other there can be no happy end to it.

– *Death in the Afternoon*, 1932

Ernest Hemingway

Prose is architecture, not interior decoration, and the Baroque is over.

– *Death in the Afternoon*, 1932

*I*f a writer of prose knows enough about what he is writing about he may omit things that he knows and the reader, if the writer is writing truly enough, will have a feeling of those things as strongly as though the writer had stated them. The dignity of movement of an ice-berg is due to only one-eighth of it being above water.

– *Death in the Afternoon*, 1932

Ernest Hemingway

*T*he great thing is to last and get your work done and see and hear and learn and understand; and write when there is something that you know; and not before; and not too damned much after.

– *Death in the Afternoon*, 1932

Ernest Hemingway

I am trying to make, before I get through, a picture of the whole world—or as much of it as I have seen. Boiling it down always, rather than spreading it out thin.

– Letter to mother-in-law Mrs. Paul Pfeiffer, Madrid, October 16, 1933

*P*aris is very beautiful this fall. It was a fine place to be quite young in and it is a necessary part of a man's education. We all loved it once and we lie if we say we didn't. But she is like a mistress who does not grow old and she has other lovers now.

– "A Paris Letter," *Esquire*, February 1934

Ernest Hemingway

*F*orget your personal tragedy. We are all bitched from the start and you especially have to be hurt like hell before you can write seriously.

– Letter to F. Scott Fitzgerald, Key West, May 28, 1934

Ernest Hemingway

*F*or any good man would rather take chances any day with his life than his livelihood and that is the main point about professionals that amateurs seem never to appreciate.

– "Notes on a Dangerous Game: The Third Tanganyika Letter," *Esquire*, July 1934

*A*ll good books are alike in that they are truer than if they had really happened and after you are finished reading one you will feel that all that happened to you and afterwards it all belongs to you; the good and the bad, the ecstasy, the remorse and sorrow, the people and the places and how the weather was.

– "Old Newsman Writes: A Letter from Cuba," *Esquire*, December 1934

*U*nlike many novels, none of the characters or incidents in this book is imaginary. Any one not finding sufficient love interest is at liberty, while reading it, to insert whatever love interest he or she may have at the time.

– *Green Hills of Africa*, 1935

*W*riters are forged in injustice as a sword is forged.

– *Green Hills of Africa*, 1935

A country, finally, erodes and the dust blows away, the people all die and none of them were of any importance permanently, except those who practiced the arts, and these now wish to cease their work because it is too lonely, too hard to do, and is not fashionable.

– *Green Hills of Africa*, 1935

They wrote in the old days that it is sweet and fitting to die for one's country. But in modern war there is nothing sweet nor fitting in your dying. You will die like a dog for no good reason.

– "Notes on the Next War: A Serious Topical Letter," *Esquire*, September 1935

There is no use writing anything that has been written before unless you can beat it. What a writer in our time has to do is write what hasn't been written before or beat dead men at what they have done.

– "Monologue to the Maestro: A High Seas Letter," *Esquire*, October 1935

*K*ilimanjaro is a snow-covered mountain 19,710 feet high, and is said to be the highest mountain in Africa. Its western summit is called the Masai "Ngaje Ngai," the House of God. Close to the western summit there is a dried and frozen carcass of a leopard. No one has explained what the leopard was seeking at that altitude.

– Epigraph, *The Snows of Kilimanjaro,* 1936

Ernest Hemingway

*I*t is a dangerous thing in a dictatorship to have a long memory.

– "Wings Always over Africa: An Ornithological Letter," *Esquire,* January 1936

Ernest Hemingway

*A*s I say am always a perfectly safe man to tell any dirt to as it goes in one ear and out my mouth.

– Letter to John Dos Passos, Key West, April 12, 1937

There is only one form of government that cannot produce good writers, and that system is fascism. For fascism is a lie told by bullies. A writer who will not lie cannot live or work under fascism.

– "Fascism Is a Lie," speech delivered to the American Writers Congress, New York City, June 4, 1937

We know war is bad. Yet sometimes it is necessary to fight. But still war is bad and any man who says it is not is a liar. But it is very complicated and difficult to write about truly.

– Letter to Russian critic Ivan Kashkin, Key West, March 23, 1939

But then writing is a very far fetched business and to be a writer you have to write even though you have to go far away or wait a long time to fetch the truth.

– "The Writer as a Writer," *Directions*, May-June 1939

There is nothing else than now. There is neither yesterday, certainly, nor is there any tomorrow. How old must you be before you know that? There is only now, and if now is only two days, then two days is your life and everything in it will be in proportion. This is how you live a life in two days. And if you stop complaining and asking for what you never will get, you will have a good life.
– *For Whom the Bell Tolls*, 1940

No animal has more liberty than the cat, but it buries the mess it makes. The cat is the best anarchist.
– *For Whom the Bell Tolls*, 1940

Today is only one day in all the days that will ever be. But what will happen in all the other days that ever come can depend on what you do today.
– *For Whom the Bell Tolls*, 1940

*T*he world is a fine place and worth the fighting for and I hate very much to leave it.
– *For Whom the Bell Tolls*, 1940

*M*y temptation is always to write too much. I keep it under control so as not to have to cut out crap and re-write. Guys who think they are geniuses because they have never learned to say no to a typewriter are a common phenomenon.
– Letter to Maxwell Perkins, La Finca Vigia, San Francisco de Paula, Cuba, February 1940

I have to write to be happy whether I get paid for it or not. But it is a hell of a disease to be born with. I like to do it. Which is even worse. That makes it from a disease into a vice. Then I want to do it better than anybody has ever done it which makes it into an obsession.
– Letter to publisher Charles Scribner, Havana, February 24, 1940

*A*ll my life I've looked at words as though I were seeing them for the first time.
– Letter to fiancée Mary Welsh, La Finca Vigia, April 9, 1945

I hate to kill a day when I could live it.
– Letter to ex-wife Hadley Mowrer, La Finca Vigia, April 24, 1945

*I*t wasn't by accident that the Gettysburg address was so short. The laws of prose writing are as immutable as those of flight, of mathematics, of physics.
– Letter to Maxwell Perkins, La Finca Vigia, July 23, 1945

*I*t's this way, see—when a writer first starts out, he gets a big kick from the stuff he does, and the reader doesn't get any; then, after a while, the writer gets a little kick and the reader gets a little kick; and, finally, if the writer's any good, he doesn't get any kick at all. The reader gets everything.
– "Indestructible," profile in the *New Yorker*, January 4, 1947

I'd have to work and try to write well if I were in jail, or if I had 20 million dollars or if I was broke and working at something else to keep going, or if I was going to die, or if I had word I was going to live forever.

– Letter to Charles Scribner, La Finca Vigia, June 28, 1947

Ernest Hemingway

A writer has no more right to inform the public of the weaknesses and strengths of his fellow professionals than a doctor or lawyer has. Writers should stick together like wolves or gypsies and they are fools to attack each other to please the people who would exploit or destroy them.

– "Hemingway in the Afternoon," interview in *Time,* August 4, 1947

Ernest Hemingway

*T*he fact the book was a tragic one did not make me unhappy since I believed that life was a tragedy and knew it could only have one end. But finding you were able to make something up; to create truly enough so that it made you happy to read it; and to do this every day you worked was something that gave a greater pleasure than any I had ever known. Beside it nothing else mattered.

– *A Farewell to Arms,* 1948 edition

*Y*our legend grows like the barnacles on
the bottom of a ship and is about as useful.
Less Usefull.
– Letter to writer Lillian Ross, La Finca Vigia, July 28, 1948

*A*nd how do you like it *now*, Gentlemen?
– Letter to Charles Scribner, La Finca Vigia, August 27, 1949

I believe that basically you write for two people:
yourself to try to make it absolutely perfect; or if
not that then wonderful. Then you write for who
you love whether she can read or write or not
and whether she is alive or dead.
– Letter to biographer and literary critic Arthur Mizener, La Finca Vigia,
   May 12, 1950

Writing and travel broaden your ass if not your mind and I like to write standing up.

– Letter to *New York Times Book Review* columnist Harvey Breit,
  La Finca Vigia, July 9, 1950

Ernest Hemingway

Politics I would rather not be quoted on. All the contact I have had with it has left me feeling as though I had been drinking out of spittoons.

– "Talk with Mr. Hemingway," interview with Harvey Breit, *New York
  Times Book Review*, September 17, 1950

Ernest Hemingway

The critic, out on a limb, is more fun to see than a mountain lion. The critic gets paid for it so it is so much more just that he should be out on that limb than the poor cat who does it for nothing.

– Statement in "Success, It's Wonderful" by Harvey Breit, *New York
  Times Book Review*, December 3, 1950

*M*y own ethics are only to attack on time and never leave your woundeds except to pleasant auspices.

– Letter to writer A. E. Hotchner, La Finca Vigia, January 5, 1951

Ernest Hemingway

*T*his is the prose that I have been working for all my life that should read easily and simply and seem short and yet have all the dimensions of the visible world and the world of a man's spirit.

– On *The Old Man and the Sea*, letter to Charles Scribner, La Finca Vigia, October 5, 1951

Ernest Hemingway

"*A*ge is my alarm clock."

– Santiago in *The Old Man and the Sea*, 1952

Ernest Hemingway

"*A* man can be destroyed but not defeated."

– Santiago in *The Old Man and the Sea*, 1952

Ernest Hemingway

"*N*ow is no time to think of what you do not have. Think of what you can do with what there is."

– Santiago in *The Old Man and the Sea*, 1952

I cannot write beautifully but I can write with great accuracy (sometimes; I hope) and the accuracy makes a sort of beauty.

– Letter to art historian Bernard Berenson, La Finca Vigia, Cuba, March 20, 1953

Ernest Hemingway

A ctually if a writer needs a dictionary he should not write. He should have read the dictionary at least three times from beginning to end and then have loaned it to someone who needs it.

– Letter to Bernard Berenson, La Finca Vigia, Cuba, March 20, 1953

Ernest Hemingway

Y ou can write any time people will leave you alone and not interrupt you. Or rather you can if you will be ruthless enough about it.

– "Ernest Hemingway, The Art of Fiction #21," interview with George Plimpton, *Paris Review*, May 1954

Ernest Hemingway

T he fun of talk is to explore, but much of it and all that is irresponsible should not be written. Once written you have to stand by it. You may have said it to see whether you believed it or not.

– "Ernest Hemingway, The Art of Fiction #21," interview with George Plimpton, *Paris Review*, May 1954

I still believe, though, that it is very bad for a writer to talk about how he writes. He writes to be read by the eye and no explanations or dissertations should be necessary. You can be sure that there is much more there than will be read at any first reading and having made this it is not the writer's province to explain it or to run guided tours through the more difficult country of his work.

– "Ernest Hemingway, The Art of Fiction #21," interview with George Plimpton, *Paris Review*, May 1954

You know that fiction, prose rather, is possibly the roughest trade of all in writing. You do not have the reference, the old important reference. You have the sheet of blank paper, the pencil, and the obligation to invent truer than things can be true. You have to take what is not palpable and make it completely palpable and also have it seem normal and so that it can become part of the experience of the person who reads it.

– Letter to Bernard Berenson, La Finca Vigia, Cuba, September 24, 1954

Writing, at its best, is a lonely life....For he does his work alone and if he is a good enough writer he must face eternity, or the lack of it, each day.
– Nobel Prize acceptance statement, December 10, 1954

For a true writer each book should be a new beginning where he tries again for something that is beyond attainment. He should always try for something that has never been done or that others have tried and failed. Then sometimes, with great luck, he will succeed.
– Nobel Prize acceptance statement, December 10, 1954

How simple the writing of literature would be if it were only necessary to write in another way what has been well written. It is because we have had such great writers in the past that a writer is driven far out past where he can go, out to where no one can help him.
– Nobel Prize acceptance statement, December 10, 1954

*N*o good book has ever been written that has in it symbols arrived at beforehand and stuck in. That kind of symbol sticks out like—like raisins in raisin bread. Raisin bread is all right, but plain bread is better.

– "Hemingway in Cuba," interview with Robert Manning, *Atlantic Monthly*, December 1954

*W*hen you're a writer, you got to keep it going, because when you've lost it God knows when you'll get it back.

– "Dropping in on Hemingway," interview by Lloyd Lockhart, *Toronto Star Weekly Magazine*, April 1958

*I*f I knew then what I know now I would have written my books under an assumed name. I don't want to be famous. I don't like publicity. All I ask from life is to write, hunt, fish, and be obscure.

– "Dropping in on Hemingway," interview by Lloyd Lockhart, *Toronto Star Weekly Magazine*, April 1958

*I*f you are lucky enough to have lived in Paris
as a young man, then wherever you go for
the rest of your life, it stays with you, for Paris
is a moveable feast.
– *A Moveable Feast*, published posthumously, 1964

Ernest Hemingway

I would stand and look out over the roofs of
Paris and think, "Do not worry. You have always
written before and you will write now. All you
have to do is write one true sentence. Write the
truest sentence you know."
– *A Moveable Feast*, published posthumously, 1964

Ernest Hemingway

*W*ork could cure almost anything, I believed
then, and I believe now.
– *A Moveable Feast*, published posthumously, 1964

Ernest Hemingway

*I*t was all part of the fight against poverty that
you never win except by not spending.
– *A Moveable Feast*, published posthumously, 1964

*I*f a man liked his friends' painting or writing, I thought it was probably like those people who like their families, and it was not polite to criticize them. Sometimes you can go quite a long time before you criticize families, your own or those by marriage, but it is easier with bad painters because they do not do terrible things and make intimate harm as families can do. With bad painters all you need to do is not look at them.

– *A Moveable Feast*, published posthumously, 1964

*W*hen you have two people who love each other, are happy and gay and really good work is being done by one or both of them, people are drawn to them as surely as migrating birds are drawn at night to a powerful beacon.

– *A Moveable Feast*, published posthumously, 1964

*W*hen you stop doing things for fun you might as well be dead.

– *True at First Light*, published posthumously in his centennial year, 1999